OMAD COOKBOOK

40+Salad, Side dishes and pasta recipes for a healthy and balanced OMAD diet

TABLE OF CONTENTS

Committee of Publishers and Associations.

Introduction

OMAD recipes for personal enjoyment but also for family enjoyment. You will love them for sure for how easy it is to prepare them.

SIDE DISHES

SPICY SHRIMP STIR FRY

Serves: **1**

Prep Time: **10**   Minutes

Cook Time: **10**   Minutes

Total Time: **20**   Minutes

INGREDIENTS

- 1 orange
- Cayenne powder
- 3 oz shrimp
- Ginger powder
- 4 tbs vegetable stock
- Curry powder
- 25 cups red onion
- 1 cup cabbage
- Garlic powder

DIRECTIONS

1. Coat the shrimp in the seasonings.
2. Pour the broth into a pan, then add cabbage, onion, and shrimp.
3. Cook until the shrimp turns pink.
4. Serve topped with orange juice and orange slices.

Serves: **6-8**

Prep Time: **10**   Minutes

Cook Time: **15**   Minutes

Total Time: **25**   Minutes

INGREDIENTS

- 1 pizza crust
- 1 garlic clove
- ½ lb. spinach
- ½ lb. soft cheese
- 2 oz. artichoke hearts
- 1 cup mozzarella cheese
- 1 tablespoon olive oil

DIRECTIONS

1. Spread tomato sauce on the pizza crust
2. Place all the toppings on the pizza crust
3. Bake the pizza at 425 F for 12-15 minutes
4. When ready remove pizza from the oven and serve

MINT PIZZA

Serves: **6-8**

Prep Time: **10**   Minutes

Cook Time: **15**   Minutes

Total Time: **25**   Minutes

INGREDIENTS

- 1 pizza crust
- 1 olive oil
- 1 garlic clove
- 1 cup mozzarella cheese
- 2 oz. mint
- 2 courgettes

DIRECTIONS

1. Spread tomato sauce on the pizza crust
2. Place all the toppings on the pizza crust
3. Bake the pizza at 425 F for 12-15 minutes
4. When ready remove pizza from the oven and serve

SAUSAGE PIZZA

Serves: **6-8**

Prep Time: **10**   Minutes

Cook Time: **15**   Minutes

Total Time: **25**   Minutes

INGREDIENTS

- 2 pork sausages
- 1 tablespoon olive oil
- 2 garlic cloves
- 1 tsp fennel seeds
- ½ lb. ricotta
- 1 cup mozzarella cheese
- 1 oz. parmesan cheese
- 1 pizza crust

DIRECTIONS

1. Spread tomato sauce on the pizza crust
2. Place all the toppings on the pizza crust
3. Bake the pizza at 425 F for 12-15 minutes
4. When ready remove pizza from the oven and serve

BEEF & BROCCOLI STIR FRY

Serves: **4**

Prep Time: **10** Minutes

Cook Time: **30** Minutes

Total Time: **40** Minutes

INGREDIENTS

- 2 cloves garlic
- ½ lb Beef Sirloin steaks
- Chicken broth
- 2 tbs liquid Aminos
- 1 tsp onion powder
- 1 tbs parsley
- 2 cups broccoli florets

DIRECTIONS

1. Sauté the beef in a few tbs of chicken broth until brown.
2. Add onion powder, garlic, broccoli, liquid aminos and parsley.
3. Saute until well done.
4. Serve immediately.

GINGER CHICKEN SOUP

Serves: *1*

Prep Time: *5*   Minutes

Cook Time: *15*   Minutes

Total Time: *20*   Minutes

INGREDIENTS

- 2 cloves garlic
- Salt
- Pepper
- 3 stalks celery
- 3 oz chicken tenders
- 4 cups chicken broth
- 4 slices ginger

DIRECTIONS

1. Bring the broth to a boil.
2. Add the garlic, ginger, and celery.
3. Simmer for 5 minutes.
4. Add in the chicken and boil for 10 more minutes.
5. Season with salt and pepper.
6. Serve immediately.

CILANTRO SKEWERS

Serves: **1**

Prep Time: **20**   Minutes

Cook Time: **120**   Minutes

Total Time: **140**   Minutes

INGREDIENTS

- Cherry tomatoes
- Red pepper flakes
- Salt
- Pepper
- 2 tbs lemon juice
- Cilantro
- 100g shrimp

DIRECTIONS

1. Mix the cilantro, red pepper flakes, salt, pepper and shrimp together.
2. Marinade for at least 2 hours.
3. Place on skewers alternating with tomatoes.
4. Cook on a barbeque.
5. Season with salt and pepper.
6. Serve immediately.

CURRY SHRIMP

Serves: **14**

Prep Time: **10**   Minutes

Cook Time: **10**   Minutes

Total Time: **20**   Minutes

INGREDIENTS

- 1/8 cup water
- 100g shrimp
- 1 onion
- Pepper
- 1/ tsp curry powder
- ¼ tsp cumin
- Salt
- 4 garlic cloves

DIRECTIONS

1. Cook the garlic and onion until translucent.
2. Add in the shrimp, seasonings and water.
3. Cook until done.
4. Serve immediately.

Serves: *1*

Prep Time: *10* Minutes

Cook Time: *15* Minutes

Total Time: *25* Minutes

INGREDIENTS

- 100g orange roughy fillet
- 2 tbs lemon juice
- 1 tsp thyme
- 1 tsp rosemary
- ¼ tsp onion powder
- Salt
- Pepper

DIRECTIONS

1. Place the ingredients in a baking dish and cover with tin foil.
2. Bake at 350F for 15 minutes.
3. Serve hot.

Serves: *1*

Prep Time: *10*   Minutes

Cook Time: *20*   Minutes

Total Time: *30*   Minutes

INGREDIENTS

- ¼ cup lemon juice
- 1 lemon zest
- 100g tilapia
- 1 tbs onion
- 1 tsp dill
- Salt
- Pepper

DIRECTIONS

1. Place the ingredients in a tin foil, then wrap them up.
2. Cook on a grill until done
3. Serve when ready

MEDITERRANEAN SEA BASS

Serves: *1*
Prep Time: *10*   Minutes

Cook Time: *10*   Minutes

Total Time: *20*   Minutes

INGREDIENTS

- 100g sea Bass
- 2 cloves garlic
- 1 lemon juice
- 1 lemon zest
- 1 tbs onion
- ½ tsp parsley
- Salt
- Pepper

DIRECTIONS

1. Place the ingredients in a tin foil bag.
2. Cook on the barbeque for 10 minutes.
3. Serve topped with fresh parsley.

Serves: *1*
Prep Time: *10*   Minutes

Cook Time: *5*   Minutes

Total Time: *15*   Minutes

INGREDIENTS

- ½ tsp ginger
- 100g whitefish
- 1 tbs mustard
- 1 tsp wasabi powder

DIRECTIONS

1. Mix the mustard with the wasabi powder.
2. Add the ginger.
3. Coat the fish with the mixture.
4. Allow to sit for at least half an hour.
5. Grill for 5 minutes.
6. Serve hot.

CAJUN CHICKEN

Serves: *1*

Prep Time: *5*   Minutes

Cook Time: *25*   Minutes

Total Time: *30*   Minutes

INGREDIENTS

- ½ tbs milk
- ½ tsp Cajun seasoning
- 100g chicken

DIRECTIONS

1. Preheat the oven to 350F.
2. Coat the chicken with milk.
3. Sprinkle with Cajun seasoning.
4. Bake for 25 minutes.
5. Serve immediately.

BASIL CHICKEN SANDWICH

Serves: **1**

Prep Time: **5** Minutes

Cook Time: **0** Minutes

Total Time: **5** Minutes

INGREDIENTS

- ½ tomato
- 1 toast
- 100g chicken
- Basil
- Salt
- Pepper

DIRECTIONS

1. Cook the chicken, allow to chill, then shred.
2. Arrange the ingredients on top of the toast.
3. Serve immediately.

MARINARA CHICKEN

Serves: **1**

Prep Time: **10**   Minutes

Cook Time: **25**   Minutes

Total Time: **35**   Minutes

INGREDIENTS

- ½ tsp oregano
- Parsley
- 100g chicken
- 1 toast
- ½ tsp basil
- 3 garlic cloves
- 2 tsp onion
- Salt
- Pepper

DIRECTIONS

1. Crush the toast and combine with oregano, basil, salt, and pepper.
2. Coat the chicken with the mixture and place in a casserole dish.
3. Cook covered for 25 minutes at 375F.
4. Serve topped with marinara sauce and parsley.

EDAMAME FRITATTA

Serves: **2**

Prep Time: **10** Minutes

Cook Time: **20** Minutes

Total Time: **30** Minutes

INGREDIENTS

- 1 cup edamame
- 1 tablespoon olive oil
- ½ red onion
- 2 eggs
- ¼ tsp salt
- 2 oz. cheddar cheese
- 1 garlic clove
- ¼ tsp dill

DIRECTIONS

1. In a bowl whisk eggs with salt and cheese
2. In a frying pan heat olive oil and pour egg mixture
3. Add remaining ingredients and mix well
4. Serve when ready

LEEKS FRITATTA

Serves: *2*

Prep Time: *10*   Minutes

Cook Time: *20*   Minutes

Total Time: *30*   Minutes

INGREDIENTS

- ½ lb. leek
- 1 tablespoon olive oil
- ½ red onion
- ¼ tsp salt
- 2 eggs
- 2 oz. cheddar cheese
- 1 garlic clove
- ¼ tsp dill

DIRECTIONS

1. In a bowl whisk eggs with salt and cheese
2. In a frying pan heat olive oil and pour egg mixture
3. Add remaining ingredients and mix well
4. Serve when ready

Serves: **2**

Prep Time: **10**   Minutes

Cook Time: **20**   Minutes

Total Time: **30**   Minutes

INGREDIENTS

- ½ lb. mushrooms
- 1 tablespoon olive oil
- ½ red onion
- ¼ tsp salt
- 2 eggs
- 2 oz. cheddar cheese
- 1 garlic clove
- ¼ tsp dill

DIRECTIONS

1. In a bowl whisk eggs with salt and cheese
2. In a frying pan heat olive oil and pour egg mixture
3. Add remaining ingredients and mix well
4. Serve when ready

PEAS FRITATTA

Serves: **2**

Prep Time: **10**   Minutes

Cook Time: **20**   Minutes

Total Time: **30**   Minutes

INGREDIENTS

- 1 cup peas
- 1 tablespoon olive oil
- ½ red onion
- ¼ tsp salt
- 2 eggs
- 2 oz. cheddar cheese
- 1 garlic clove
- ¼ tsp dill

DIRECTIONS

1. In a bowl whisk eggs with salt and cheese
2. In a frying pan heat olive oil and pour egg mixture
3. Add remaining ingredients and mix well
4. Serve when ready.

BELL PEPPER FRITATTA

Serves: **2**

Prep Time: **10** Minutes

Cook Time: **20** Minutes

Total Time: **30** Minutes

INGREDIENTS

- 1 cup red bell pepper
- 1 tablespoon olive oil
- ½ red onion
- ¼ tsp salt
- 2 eggs
- 2 oz. parmesan cheese
- 1 garlic clove
- ¼ tsp dill

DIRECTIONS

1. In a bowl whisk eggs with salt and cheese
2. In a frying pan heat olive oil and pour egg mixture
3. Add remaining ingredients and mix well
4. Serve when ready.

POTATO FRITATTA

Serves: *2*

Prep Time: *10*   Minutes

Cook Time: *20*   Minutes

Total Time: *30*   Minutes

INGREDIENTS

- 1 cup sweet potato
- 1 tablespoon olive oil
- ½ red onion
- ¼ tsp salt
- 2 eggs
- 2 oz. cheddar cheese
- 1 garlic clove
- ¼ tsp dill

DIRECTIONS

1. In a bowl whisk eggs with salt and cheese
2. In a frying pan heat olive oil and pour egg mixture
3. Add remaining ingredients and mix well
4. Serve when ready

SKILLET PIZZA

Serves: **1**

Prep Time: **10**   Minutes

Cook Time: **20**   Minutes

Total Time: **30**   Minutes

INGREDIENTS

- ¼ red onion
- ½ cup red bell pepper
- ¼ tsp salt
- 2 eggs
- 1 cup tomato sauce
- 1 cup mozzarella cheese
- 1 pizza crust

DIRECTIONS

1. On a pizza crust spread tomato sauce
2. Add toppings on pizza
3. Place pizza in the skillet and cover with a lid
4. Cook on low heat for 18-20 minutes or until pizza is ready

GLAZED PORK CHOPS

Serves: *4*

Prep Time: *10*   Minutes

Cook Time: *15*   Minutes

Total Time: *25*   Minutes

INGREDIENTS

- 1 cup all-purpose flour
- 4 pork loin chops
- ½ cup maple syrup
- 1 tablespoon cornstarch
- 1 cup brown sugar
- pinch of salt
- 2 tablespoons water

DIRECTIONS

1. In a bowl combine salt and flour together
2. Place the pork chops in the bowl and turn to coat
3. Place pork chops in a skillet and cook until golden brown
4. Add maple syrup, sugar, water cornstarch, and bring to a boil
5. Cook until the sugar is dissolved and meat is cooked
6. When ready remove from the skillet and serve

PANINI CHICKEN

Serves: *1*

Prep Time: *10* Minutes

Cook Time: *15* Minutes

Total Time: *25* Minutes

INGREDIENTS

- 1 lb. chicken breast
- 1 tsp gingerroot
- ½ cup chicken broth
- ¼ tsp salt
- ¼ tsp turmeric
- 4 green onion

DIRECTIONS

1. In a slow cooker place your chicken and add broth, garlic clove, green onions and gingerroot
2. When ready remove chicken mixture and place the chicken on a flatbread
3. Cook sandwich in a panini maker
4. When ready remove and serve

PENNE PASTA

Serves: **2**

Prep Time: **10**   Minutes

Cook Time: **20**   Minutes

Total Time: **30**   Minutes

INGREDIENTS

- 1 package penne pasta
- 1 onion
- 1 tablespoon thyme
- 1 tablespoon basil
- ¼ cup white wine
- 1 tablespoon tomato paste
- 1 tablespoon all-purpose flour
- 1 cup parmesan cheese

DIRECTIONS

1. In a stockpot cook pasta al dente
2. In a skillet sauté onion until soft, add salt, herbs, tomato paste, flour and cook for 2-3 minutes
3. Add pasta to the tomato mixture and bring to a boil
4. When ready serve with parmesan cheese on top

TURKEY SANDWICH

Serves: *1*

Prep Time: *5*   Minutes

Cook Time: *5*   Minutes

Total Time: *10*   Minutes

INGREDIENTS

- 2 oz. cream cheese
- 2 tablespoons salad dressing
- 1 tsp garlic powder
- 1 loaf bread
- Lettuce
- 1 lb. cooked turkey
- ½ lb. swiss cheese
- 1 tomato

DIRECTIONS

1. In a bowl combine cream cheese, garlic powder and salad dressing
2. Spread mixture on the bread
3. Add lettuce, tomatoes, cheese and turkey
4. Serve when ready

Serves: *3-4*

Prep Time: *10*   Minutes

Cook Time: *20*   Minutes

Total Time: *30*   Minutes

INGREDIENTS

- 2 delicata squashes
- 2 tablespoons olive oil
- 1 tsp curry powder
- 1 tsp salt

DIRECTIONS

1. Preheat the oven to 400 F
2. Cut everything in half lengthwise
3. Toss everything with olive oil and place onto a prepared baking sheet
4. Roast for 18-20 minutes at 400 F or until golden brown
5. When ready remove from the oven and serve

BRUSSELS SPROUT CHIPS

Serves: *2*

Prep Time: *10*   Minutes

Cook Time: *20*   Minutes

Total Time: *30*   Minutes

INGREDIENTS

- 1 lb. brussels sprouts
- 1 tablespoon olive oil
- 1 tablespoon parmesan cheese
- 1 tsp garlic powder
- 1 tsp seasoning

DIRECTIONS

1. Preheat the oven to 425 F
2. In a bowl toss everything with olive oil and seasoning
3. Spread everything onto a prepared baking sheet
4. Bake for 8-10 minutes or until crisp
5. When ready remove from the oven and serve

BEET CHIPS

Serves: *2*

Prep Time: *10*   Minutes

Cook Time: *20*   Minutes

Total Time: *30*   Minutes

INGREDIENTS

- 1 lb. beet
- 1 tablespoon olive oil
- 1 tablespoon parmesan cheese
- 1 tsp garlic powder
- 1 tsp seasoning

DIRECTIONS

1. Preheat the oven to 425 F
2. In a bowl toss everything with olive oil and seasoning
3. Spread everything onto a prepared baking sheet
4. Bake for 8-10 minutes or until crisp
5. When ready remove from the oven and serve

SPINACH CHIPS

Serves: *2*
Prep Time: *10*   Minutes

Cook Time: *20*   Minutes

Total Time: *30*   Minutes

INGREDIENTS

- 1 lb. spinach
- 1 tablespoon olive oil
- 1 tablespoon parmesan cheese
- 1 tsp garlic powder
- 1 tsp seasoning

DIRECTIONS

1. Preheat the oven to 425 F
2. In a bowl toss everything with olive oil and seasoning
3. Spread everything onto a prepared baking sheet
4. Bake for 8-10 minutes or until crisp
5. When ready remove from the oven and serve

KALE CHIPS

Serves: *2*

Prep Time: *10* Minutes

Cook Time: *20* Minutes

Total Time: *30* Minutes

INGREDIENTS

- 1 lb. kale
- 1 tablespoon olive oil
- 1 tablespoon parmesan cheese
- 1 tsp garlic powder
- 1 tsp seasoning

DIRECTIONS

1. Preheat the oven to 425 F
2. In a bowl toss everything with olive oil and seasoning
3. Spread everything onto a prepared baking sheet
4. Bake for 8-10 minutes or until crisp
5. When ready remove from the oven and serve

Serves: *2*

Prep Time: *10* Minutes

Cook Time: *20* Minutes

Total Time: *30* Minutes

INGREDIENTS

- 1 lb. eggplant
- 1 tablespoon olive oil
- 1 tablespoon parmesan cheese
- 1 tsp garlic powder
- 1 tsp seasoning

DIRECTIONS

1. Preheat the oven to 425 F
2. In a bowl toss everything with olive oil and seasoning
3. Spread everything onto a prepared baking sheet
4. Bake for 8-10 minutes or until crisp
5. When ready remove from the oven and serve

TOMATO CHIPS

Serves: **2**

Prep Time: **10**   Minutes

Cook Time: **20**   Minutes

Total Time: **30**   Minutes

INGREDIENTS

- 1 lb. tomato
- 1 tablespoon olive oil
- 1 tablespoon parmesan cheese
- 1 tsp garlic powder
- 1 tsp seasoning

DIRECTIONS

1. Preheat the oven to 425 F
2. In a bowl toss everything with olive oil and seasoning
3. Spread everything onto a prepared baking sheet
4. Bake for 8-10 minutes or until crisp
5. When ready remove from the oven and serve

PASTA

SIMPLE SPAGHETTI

Serves: 2

Prep Time: 5   Minutes

Cook Time: 15   Minutes

Total Time: 20   Minutes

INGREDIENTS

- 10 oz. spaghetti
- 2 eggs
- ½ cup parmesan cheese
- 1 tsp black pepper
- Olive oil
- 1 tsp parsley
- 2 cloves garlic

DIRECTIONS

1. In a pot boil spaghetti (or any other type of pasta), drain and set aside
2. In a bowl whish eggs with parmesan cheese
3. In a skillet heat olive oil, add garlic and cook for 1-2 minutes
4. Pour egg mixture and mix well
5. Add pasta and stir well

6. When ready garnish with parsley and serve

SALAD

COUSCOUS SALAD

Serves: **5**

Prep Time: **10**   Minutes

Cook Time: **50**   Minutes

Total Time: **60**   Minutes

INGREDIENTS
Salad
- Spinach leaves
- Seasonings
- ½ pumpkin
- 1 cup cous cous
- 2 chicken breasts

Dressing
- 2 tbs vinegar
- 3 tbs olive oil
- 2 tbs mustard
- 4 tbs mayonnaise
- 2 tbs lemon juice
- Pepper
- Salt

DIRECTIONS

1. Peel and cut the pumpkin
2. Toss in oil and season
3. Roast in oven for at least 30 minutes
4. Grill the chicken
5. Cook the cous cous
6. Mix the dressing ingredients together
7. Mix everyting together in a salad bowl
8. Serve

POTATO SALAD

Serves: **2**
Prep Time: **5**   Minutes

Cook Time: **10**   Minutes

Total Time: **15**   Minutes

INGREDIENTS

- 5 potatoes
- 1 tsp cumin seeds
- 1/3 cup oil
- 2 tsp mustard
- 1 red onion
- 2 cloves garlic
- 1/3 cup lemon juice
- 1 tsp sea salt

DIRECTIONS

1. Steam the potatoes until tender
2. Mix mustard, turmeric powder, lemon juice, cumin seeds, and salt
3. Place the potatoes in a bowl and pour the lemon mixture over
4. Add the chopped onion and minced garlic over
5. Stir to coat and refrigerate covered
6. Add oil and stir before serving

CARROT SALAD

Serves: **2**

Prep Time: 5 Minutes

Cook Time: 5 Minutes

Total Time: **10** Minutes

INGREDIENTS

- 1 ½ tbs lemon juice
- 1/3 tsp salt
- ¼ tsp black pepper
- 2 tbs olive oil
- 1/3 lb carrots
- 1 tsp mustard

DIRECTIONS

1. Mix mustard, lemon juice and oil together
2. Peel and shred the carrots in a bowl
3. Stir in the dressing and season with salt and pepper
4. Mix well and allow to chill for at least 30 minutes
5. Serve

MOROCCAN SALAD

Serves: 2

Prep Time: 5   Minutes

Cook Time: 5   Minutes

Total Time: *10*   Minutes

INGREDIENTS

- 2 tbs lemon juice
- 1 tsp cumin
- 1 tsp paprika
- 3 tbs olive oil
- 2 cloves garlic
- 5 carrots
- Salt
- Pepper

DIRECTIONS

1. Peel and slice the carrots
2. Add the carrots in boiled water and simmer for at least 5 minutes
3. Drain and rinse the carrots under cold water
4. Add in a bowl
5. Mix the lemon juice, garlic, cumin, paprika, and olive oil together

6. Pour the mixture over the carrots and toss then season with salt and pepper
7. Serve immediately

AVOCADO CHICKEN SALAD

Serves: 2

Prep Time: 5   Minutes

Cook Time: 5   Minutes

Total Time: 10   Minutes

INGREDIENTS

- 3 tsp lime juice
- 3 tbs cilantro
- 1 chicken breast
- 1 avocado
- 1/3 cup onion
- 1 apple
- 1 cup celery
- Salt
- Pepper
- Olive oil

DIRECTIONS

1. Dice the chicken breast
2. Season with salt and pepper and cook into a greased skillet until golden
3. Dice the vegetables and place over the chicken in a bowl
4. Mash the avocado and sprinkle in the cilantro

5. Season with salt and pepper and add lime juice
6. Serve drizzled with olive oil

CUCUMBER SALAD

Serves: *8*

Prep Time: *5*   Minutes

Cook Time: *5*   Minutes

Total Time: *10*   Minutes

INGREDIENTS

- 2 cucumbers
- ½ cup vinegar
- 2 tsp sugar
- 1/3 cup water
- 2 tbs sour cream
- ½ tbs salt
- 1 ½ tsp paprika
- ½ onion

DIRECTIONS

1. Peel and slice the cucumbers
2. Place the cucumbers on a baking sheet and sprinkle with salt
3. Allow to chill for about 30 minutes then squeeze out the excess water
4. Place the onion slices in a bowl and add the drained cucumbers over
5. Add water, sugar, vinegar and paprika

6. Allow to marinate for at least 2 hours

7. Serve

MANGO SALAD

Serves: *4*

Prep Time: *10*   Minutes

Cook Time: *5*   Minutes

Total Time: *15*   Minutes

INGREDIENTS
Salad
- Salad leaves
- 2 chicken breasts
- 2 mangoes
- 2 avocados
- 2 tbs pine nuts

Dressing
- 3 tbs oil
- Salt
- Pepper
- 2 tbs lemon juice
- 3 tbs orange juice
- 1 tsp mustard

DIRECTIONS

1. Divide the salat onto 4 plates
2. Slice the peeled mango and place over the salad
3. Peel and slice the avocado then place it on top

4. Grill the chicken, dice it and place it over

5. Mix the dressing ingredients together and pour over

6. Serve immediately

RICE SALAD

Serves: *4*

Prep Time: *10*   Minutes

Cook Time: *5*   Minutes

Total Time: *15*   Minutes

INGREDIENTS
Salad
- 3 tbs basil leaves
- 100g Kalamata olives
- 3 tbs pine nuts
- 2 green shallots
- ½ sun dried tomato
- 1 cup rice

Dressing
- 3 tbs oil
- Pepper
- 2 tbs mustard
- 3 tbs lemon juice
- Salt
- 1 clove garlic

DIRECTIONS

1. Cook the rice
2. Mix the dressing ingredients together

3. Mix the salad ingredients with the rice in a bowl

4. Add the dressing and serve

THANK YOU FOR READING THIS BOOK!

CPSIA information can be obtained
at www.ICGtesting.com
Printed in the USA
BVHW031917160321
602656BV00004BA/62